Praise for *Vision, Diversity, and Cu*

As a college president, I am constantly looking for new ways to develop and inspire our college community. This book is truly unique as it uses a pastime enjoyable for most as a refreshing approach to leadership development.

The author uses the jigsaw puzzle to illustrate in a simple and elegant way the key components of effective leadership. She argues that, just as a jigsaw puzzle is made up of many different pieces that must fit together to create a complete picture, a successful leader must reflect with clarity the completed picture, provide all resources needed for the team to be successful, and continuously reflect that picture as needed for the progress toward completion. Of note is the author's emphasis on wellness as an integral piece of the leadership puzzle. In the demanding world of competing priorities, it's all too easy to neglect our team's well-being. The inclusion of wellness as a cornerstone of effective leadership is not just a timely reminder in today's high-stress and changing environment but also provides actionable strategies for leaders to embed well-being into their organizational culture.

What truly resonated with me is the book's inherent message: Leadership isn't about setting goals and deadlines but assembling an evolving vision with attention to every piece, acknowledging and celebrating diversity of the teams, and the infusion with intentionality of the team's personal well-being. The book is full of practical advice for leaders at all levels. For any leader, educator, or individual seeking a holistic view of leadership that emphasizes both success and wellness, this is must-read. It's more than a guide; it's an invitation to introspection and growth.

Dr. Sunem Beaton-Garcia
President, Chippewa Valley Technical College

This book is a refreshing and innovative take on leadership and management that brings a new perspective to the table. Drawing inspiration from the simple yet profound act of assembling jigsaw puzzles, Marjorie Loring manages to distill complex leadership concepts into easy digestible and relatable lessons. Get ready to embark on a transformative journey with *Vision, Diversity, and Culture*. Your leadership style will never be the same.

Connie Phelan
author, *Inspired Courage*

WOW! This book clearly defines and connects all the leadership pieces while making the roles and responsibilities very understandable. The author's comprehensive dive into the varied aspects of leadership is easy to understand and implement because they are well aligned to real life in the workplace.

Nancy Proffitt
Executive Leadership Coach,
author, *Focused Leadership*

An incredibly well-written and easy read book by two incredible professionals in their respective fields. The combination of leadership lessons with wellness and self-care advice is sorely needed for today's leaders. The take-away that I come back to daily from this book is the reminder that as a leader, I am the box top of the puzzle. No matter how well I believe I painted the vision, originally, if I am not there to continuously refresh that clear vision, it is like I took the box top away in the middle of the team trying to assemble a complex puzzle. Well done!

Marielena DeSanctis
President, Community College of Denver

Vision, Diversity, and Culture: What Jigsaw Puzzles Can Teach Us About Leadership and Management by Marjorie J. Loring is a remarkable book that offers valuable insights into the world of leadership and management. What sets this book apart is its refreshingly simple approach to leadership concepts. Loring's writing provides delightfully digestible ideas and serves as a compelling reminder of our roles as leaders.

Throughout the book, Loring emphasizes the importance of casting an inspirational vision, providing unwavering support, and never ceasing to offer sideline coaching. These principles are presented in a way that makes them not only easy to grasp but also enjoyable to implement.

Reading *Vision, Diversity, and Culture* felt like indulging in a delicious treat for the mind. Loring's engaging style and relatable examples make the learning experience enjoyable. The actionable tips provided throughout the book are the icing on the cake, giving readers practical tools to enhance their leadership skills.

I strongly recommend this book to all people leaders, whether you're a seasoned executive or just starting your leadership journey. *Vision, Diversity, and Culture* is a valuable resource that will help you become a more effective and inspiring leader. Marjorie J. Loring has crafted a book that not only educates but also entertains, making it a must-read for anyone looking to elevate their leadership game.

Sophia Galvin
Vice President, Talent and Culture, Broward College

In her thought-provoking book, *Vision, Diversity, and Culture: What Jigsaw Puzzles Can Teach Us About Leadership and Management*, Marjorie J. Loring dives into the very relatable metaphor of jigsaw puzzles and uncovers nuggets of wisdom about leadership and management. The book creatively explores how puzzles mirror the intricacies of the corporate world, providing valuable insights for leaders seeking to enhance their managerial skills. Through anecdotes, the author illustrates how assembling a puzzle involves effective delegation, strategic planning, collaboration, and adaptability which are all essential qualities for successful leadership. Engaging and informative, this book challenges readers to view puzzles not only as a leisurely pastime but also as a powerful metaphor for navigating the complexities of the modern workplace. Whether you are an experienced leader or just starting your leadership journey, this book offers a fresh perspective, equipping you with invaluable lessons to tackle challenges and lead with confidence.

Michelle Cummings
Founder, Facilitator, and Big Wheel,
Training Wheels Group, LLC

VISION, DIVERSITY, AND CULTURE

What Jigsaw Puzzles Can Teach Us About
Leadership and Management

MARJORIE J. LORING

Cover Design by Yeshua Machado Graphic Design
Illustrations by Marjorie J. Loring

PEAK PRESS

An Imprint for GracePoint Publishing (www.GracePointPublishing.com)

GracePoint Matrix, LLC
624 S. Cascade Ave, Suite 201, Colorado Springs, CO 80903
www.GracePointMatrix.com   Email: Admin@GracePointMatrix.com
SAN # 991-6032

A Library of Congress Control Number has been requested and is pending.

ISBN: (Paperback) 978-0-9992517-8-2
eISBN: 978-0-9992517-9-9

Books may be purchased for educational, business, or sales promotional use.
For bulk order requests and price schedule contact:
Orders@GracePointPublishing.com

Gratitude

For Esther, who believes that I can do anything to which I set my mind and heart and throws her full support behind me with encouragement and honest feedback every step of the way. I could not have done this without her unwavering love and support.

◈

For my program participants, who make a commitment to ongoing professional development, are open to learning from others, and are willing to share their knowledge, perspectives, and stories for the benefit of others.

◈

For my wellness contributor, Lisa, who gives so much of her heart toward bringing a more holistic and comprehensive culture of employee wellness to the workplace and to the leadership mindset.

◈

Special thanks go to Connie Phelan, Karen Pfeffer, Randolph Partain, and Judith Hoover for their feedback and suggestions during the beta reading process.

Table of Contents

Introduction

The puzzle piece is often used as a symbol of connection, individuality, belonging, and recognition. In fact, companies will often award plaques or trophies that include the image or model of a puzzle piece to recognize team members as an essential part of the organization and its success.

During the years of the pandemic, as I shifted from being a face-to-face to a fully remote program facilitator, one habit I developed to clear my head was taking mini breaks and working on jigsaw puzzles. As the months went by, doing these puzzles revealed a variety of insights that I thought would be fun to include in my leadership training sessions. I shared a few of the insights during one session and was encouraged by how the participants related to them. These simple but practical concepts were embraced enthusiastically, stimulating connection and lively discussion within the group. That was when my wellness contributor, Dr. Lisa Elsinger, encouraged me to give these lessons a bigger platform.

Recognizing that the concepts revealed through each puzzle insight are only part of the solution to being an effective leader, I asked her to join me on this journey by contributing an employee wellness perspective which is a key element of effective leadership practices. These combined perspectives, leadership lessons, and employee wellness, is what I share with you in this book.

Working within the theme of the jigsaw puzzle, these insights help guide leaders (supervisors and managers) with simple straightforward concepts that when put into practice will inspire a healthy work environment where teams can thrive.

Each concept will include:

> Puzzle Insight
> What Does This Teach Us about Leadership?
> Wellness Perspective
> Challenge: Leadership in Action

When we find ourselves face-to-face with any challenge that comes our way, it will be the adaptable and agile teams who create a new normal together and innovate new possibilities for the future. What we carry forward from the concepts in this book are the perspectives we gain and share and how we, as leaders, are changed for the better by them.

If you are a leader, or are planning to become one, this book will take you on a journey that will sharpen your insight on goals and guidelines (Vision), broaden your perspective on work and processes (Diversity), and open you to new ways of understanding, supporting, and celebrating the people you lead and the environment you help create (Culture).

Each insight ends with a specific challenge for putting what you learn into practice. By taking the time to turn new insight into action, you will be creating and maintaining an environment that increases team member loyalty, engagement, and productivity, reduces stress to manageable levels, and prevents the burnout that all too often results in team member turnover.

Let's get started.

Part One

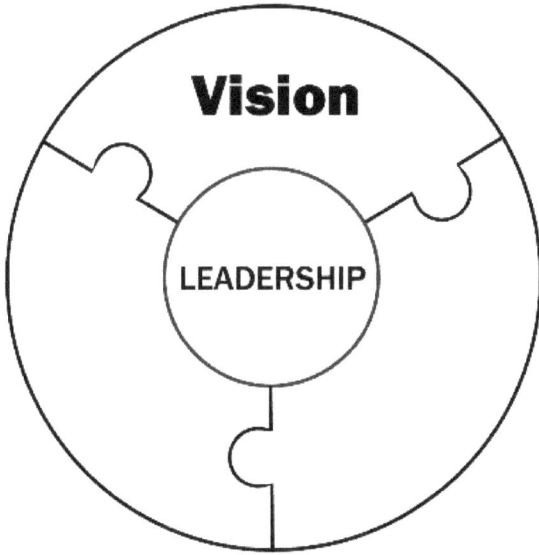

Vision

LEADERSHIP

A vision is something we can see; however, to visualize means to imagine what something looks like in our mind's eye. It can be a product, a service, or an impact to meet a need or fill a void. Whatever it is, it must take some kind of shape, form, or characteristic that can be easily visualized, identified, and recognized.

When we determine that our organization's vision is to have the best product, provide the best service, or have the greatest impact, we have fallen short of coming up with a true vision because we haven't clarified what any of these things look like. Instead, we have articulated a hopeful end result for something that lacks visual characteristics.

If leaders want to bring people on board who will be excited about helping a vision become a reality, the first step is to help them see what they are working toward with clarity and focus.

Make sure that what you see is what they get.

Included in Part One:

The Big Picture

Start with an Easy Win

Establish Guidelines

Organize and Assess

Milestones Matter

The Big Picture

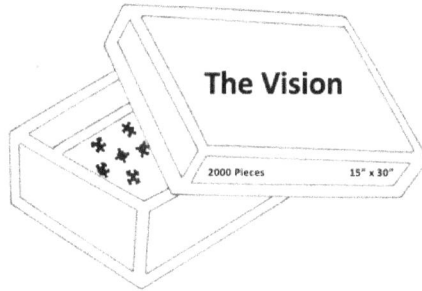

The Puzzle Box Is the Guide

Dumping puzzle pieces from the box onto a table can be a bit overwhelming. This is often what a new work assignment or project feels like. As leaders, we need to provide the context. In the case of the jigsaw puzzle, it is the box cover that gives the context of the project. While we do not yet know how easy or difficult it will be or how much help will be needed, the image of what the completed puzzle looks like, the number of pieces that must be put in place, and the shape and size of the completed work are all made clear before we begin.

When you open a jigsaw puzzle and empty the pieces onto a table, what do you do with the box? Well, personally, I place the box cover off to the side of my work area so I can keep an eye on the image. It is important that I maintain clarity about the end goal which means that even as I shift my attention to the individual pieces and sections, I can stay mindful of the bigger picture.

As a leader and the team vision holder, YOU are the puzzle box!

You provide clarity on what "done" looks like. When assigning a project or task, you are responsible for providing the context so that team members can easily see the bigger picture of their efforts. Simon Sinek, author and inspirational speaker, shares,

> *"I am often surprised how many visionary leaders assume that because their vision is clear to them it's clear to everyone else in the organization. Which of course it's not."* [1]

Leaders need to clearly communicate what "done" looks like and give team members the freedom to complete the tasks involved while also maintaining a consistent presence in case they need additional input or clarification. When you are not available, it is like taking the puzzle box cover away. Keep in mind how much more difficult it can be to work on a jigsaw puzzle if the completed image is kept out of sight.

Notice how I said that I set the puzzle box cover off to the side. If I put it right in the middle of my work area it would be in my way.

> As a leader and the team vision holder, YOU are the puzzle box!

The same goes for leaders. Maintaining a presence does not mean you have to stay right in the middle of things (micromanaging is counterproductive), but neither does it mean being invisible. Rather, it means that you are always available on the sidelines in case you are needed, and you will check in now and then to lend a hand or show your support! My puzzle box cover doesn't stay firmly in place off to the side. Sometimes it needs to be closer for enhanced clarity.

Regularly doing a walk-through of the work area is a great way to show your employees that you are available. You can ask them how they are doing with the project and initiate casual (non-work-related) conversations. Team members can take advantage of this opportunity to ask questions they might not have been comfortable asking by showing up at your office. Your willingness to answer these questions solidifies the impression that you are interested and approachable. Being available on the sidelines is good, but maintaining a presence and going to your team members now and then rather than making them come to you helps establish an environment of openness and collaboration.

The important thing to remember about the big picture of a project or goal is that team members often work on different parts of the whole. If a team member does not see how their efforts fit into the bigger picture, they may lose motivation and feel as if they are spending time on less important work. By recognizing each role and task as equally critical to the big picture and acknowledging the importance of every piece that falls into place, you are affirming the value of their efforts and motivating them forward.

This lesson emerged as I put together the pieces of a perfectly landscaped house on a lake. I noticed it had a garden by the entrance gate, a brick walkway, and just past the side yard was a sailboat docked in the lake behind the house. Because I have the box cover with the completed image, my end goal or what done looks like is clear. I see how the landscape is laid out and I feel comfortable as I begin placement of the pieces within each area. Each section makes sense within the bigger picture and is a critical part of the scene. Working on the garden is just as important as working on the house, the sailboat, or the walkway.

Leaders must also understand that an important part of the big picture is providing adequate resources.

Imagine my puzzle as an assigned work project. If I am going to do the puzzle successfully, I expect to have the following resources available:

1. A table big enough to fit my completed puzzle.

2. An additional area large enough (or a series of trays) to lay out and organize the pieces that have not yet been put into place.
3. Adequate lighting.

What happens if I do not have access to these resources?

I try my best to find ways to complete the puzzle by innovating and trying to be creative with the resources I do have. I can do some of the following:

- Find and section off an area of the floor to assemble the puzzle.
- Leave the unassembled pieces in the box and sift through them to find the pieces I need.
- Seek out a teammate who is willing and available to help.
- Communicate my plan to the rest of the team to make them aware of the challenges and ask for their support.

Am I set up for success? Maybe.

With the appropriate support from both the team leader and my teammates (respect of space, teamwork, flex time, additional breaks as needed, and extended deadlines) success is possible. But at what cost? Leaders who compensate for a lack of adequate resources by relying on team member innovation are taking a serious risk.

What could happen in my puzzle scenario:

- My stress level increases because of an inadequate work-space and the potential for lost puzzle pieces.
- The process of looking for the puzzle pieces in the box slows down my progress, adding additional stress about meeting the target deadline.
- Teammates who are assigned other priorities are not able to help as much as anticipated.

- Working on the floor is causing physical issues with my neck, back, and legs. The physical pain, stress, frustration, and the slow pace of progress begins to discourage me.
- I lose my motivation, my attitude begins to suffer, and I start to blame leadership for putting me in an impossible situation. I may even start looking for another job.

> An important part of the big picture is providing adequate resources.

What Does This Teach Us about Leadership?

Leaders should understand that even when employees are ready and willing to help achieve goals, that even the most reliable and innovative ones can lose their motivation if they are not provided purpose, outcome clarity, guide-on-the-side support, proper training when needed, and adequate resources as these are all critical for achieving team member commitment and big picture success.

While all resources are important, there is one resource that is often overlooked by leaders: providing opportunities for employees to attend professional development and skill building programs. Too often I have heard employees say they are unable to get approval from their supervisor to attend training programs because the department is too busy for them to be away. I often wonder why actively training and upskilling employees is not considered a critical component of regular business operations. Whether it is a new or updated business application, training for re-certification, or just a desire to work on improving soft skill competencies, investing time for ongoing learning helps ensure that competence levels stay up to date and in line with how a particular industry faces the big picture challenges ahead.

Wellness Perspective

We spend a great deal of time at work, whether we work on-site, remotely from home, or a hybrid arrangement of the two. A leader sets the stage for the team member's experience, which includes the work expectations and the work environment. Degree of presence and quality of interaction are equally important in creating a positive experience that helps avoid miscommunication and reduce stress while keeping people focused on tasks at hand and working toward the outcome or deliverable. A clear understanding of the big picture creates a feeling of being connected to department goals— a sense of being more than a cog in the wheel, but an important contributor to the organization's mission.

We have learned that leaders who display trust and provide some autonomy to their team members often observe a greater degree of diligence and dedication, along with higher quality work. The Self-Determination Theory, which describes factors influencing motivation, posits that people are more likely to be motivated if they have a sense of control over their actions. Providing adequate resources plays a key role in this success. When we have the necessary tools and resources, we can achieve a higher level of competence, which leads to a sense of accomplishment. A positive experience at work contributes to a positive organizational culture by empowering individuals and creating collaborative teams.[2]

Remind them that they are not alone.

When getting ready to embark on any new endeavor, the following questions run through my mind:

- What do I want to accomplish?
- Am I up for the challenge?
- Do I believe I can do it?
- How long is it going to take?
- Do I have everything I need? What if I do not?

- Will I need/get help? If yes, then from whom?
- What happens if I fail?

These are great questions to remember when assigning a project and delegating tasks to team members. They make great project planning discussion questions when you change the *I* to *We*!

Challenge: The Big Picture

Look at either a project/task you have recently assigned, or one you plan to assign.

1. Write down how you will define the big picture (What does the successful outcome of your expectation look like?) and how you will share your availability as a guide on the side.
2. Describe how each team member's role plays a critical part of the big picture and who will benefit from the expected outcome (this interjects purpose).
3. What resources do you believe are critical in supporting success? Plan for and provide opportunities for training.
4. Ask your team if they need additional resources from the ones provided and encourage them to come to you if any additional needs surface as they move forward. Look for ways to provide these resources.
5. Acknowledge the resources you are unable to provide and discuss with your team the ways it could impact the process, timeline, and potential for success. Innovate solutions together and adjust expectations and goals.

Start with an Easy Win

The First Thing You Accomplish Connects You to the Big Picture

When doing a jigsaw puzzle, I often start by finding and setting aside the edge pieces. The edges are easier to find in the mix and provide an immediate sense of forward movement toward my goal. The edges will provide the "You are Here" orientation markers for the rest of the process. Depending on the puzzle, I might also start by sorting the pieces by color or pattern. Getting off to a good start initiates real engagement. The initial progress made by these easy wins encourages and motivates me and before you know it, I am all in.

In one puzzle, the edges were easy to find because they all shared a thick red line on the edge of the border. Another puzzle had a picture of assorted trays and each one was filled with a different color of buttons. The process of sorting the puzzle pieces by color made it feel like things were progressing even before I put the first piece in place! These easy wins kept me motivated.

Making progress one step or (one piece) at a time convinces me that this is going to happen because I am clear

> Getting off to a good start initiates real engagement.

on the vision, know where I am going, and have a plan on how I am going to get there. That first step into an easy win is the most important one to take because it aligns my motivation with the big picture.

I can see how true this is for me whenever I get an idea for a new training program or team building event. As soon as I take the first step and put the idea into an outline, my enthusiasm increases, I get a rush of excitement, and I can feel my creative juices kicking into gear. The best part is seeing how my team catches the wave and joins me in moving my idea forward.

What Does This Teach Us about Leadership?

If you want your team to engage with your vision, you need to show them that you are "all in." You cannot just dump a pile of work, a big picture, and a deadline onto their plates without allowing time to discuss ways to get started. Have a brainstorming session to give them time to come up with some ideas for easy wins. An important thing I learned about group discussion is that when leaders offer their own ideas first, it often shuts down contributions from team members who tend to fall in line behind that idea. Instead, add your thoughts to the mix later in the discussion. Taking the time with your team at the beginning of a project and recognizing the small wins at the onset sends a clear message that you want them to start out on the right track, that you trust them to take it from there, and that you are available to help them if they get stuck. This simple act of leadership triggers the initiative that fuels the initial forward movement, strengthens collaboration, and supports further progress.

This "all in" strategy came into play while working on the development of a new leadership program. Our area was charged with developing a leadership course around a newly adopted set of performance appraisal measurements. I had a purpose (the big picture), a program calendar outline (my first easy win), and I was excited to get the team involved and the project going. I quickly recognized that the scope of the proposed twenty-four-week program was a bit overwhelming to my team. They struggled with where to start with researching, selecting, and organizing what would become the program content. I had my own ideas but resisted sharing my thoughts. It was too soon in the process. Instead, I assigned them to sub-teams that would focus on different aspects of the course outline (course structure, learning platform, lesson formats and assessments, guest facilitators, and inclusion of external resources). Each sub-team was then given time to discuss how they could build their part of the big picture by coming up with their first easy wins. At the next meeting, ideas were shared and integrated while I watched the enthusiasm build. They didn't need to start out with my ideas. What a loss it would have been had they not been given the opportunity to tap into their own creative minds. My role as their leader was to help guide the emerging ideas into a cohesive plan. In this example, multiple easy wins would happen simultaneously, and I watched as project engagement kicked into high gear.

In a Leadership Now article by author and leadership coach, Michael McKinney, he states,

> *"[B]y highlighting small-wins you help to create the kind of abundance-thinking needed for growth and forward momentum. A strategy of small-wins helps to develop the kind of outlook associated with abundance-thinking, self-efficacy, hope, optimism, and resilience."* [3]

Easy wins come in varying ways, but the feeling of accomplishment is crucial in maintaining engagement, confidence, and forward progress.

Wellness Perspective

When embarking on any new project, early wins promote a sense of self-efficacy, which is the belief in one's ability to perform an activity or succeed in a particular situation. Having small wins at the early stages of a project is important because it leads to the brain's release of the neurochemical dopamine which creates the feel-good emotions that increase motivation, direct our focus, and make us want to achieve more.

Celebrating initial accomplishments (even with a simple high five and an energetic yes!) can also lead to enthusiasm to work toward even bigger goals. When leaders acknowledge a team's progress, morale gets a boost and people feel encouraged as the project progresses.

Challenge: Easy Wins

Look at either a project you have recently assigned, or one you plan to assign.

1. List what you see as potential easy wins for the project.
2. Facilitate a discussion of what might be easy wins from the perspective of the team members.
3. Share your list and let them decide what works best for them.

Be sure to recognize and high five the easy wins when they happen.

Establish Guidelines

Framing and Setting Boundaries

Since one of my first easy wins is often finding the edge pieces of my puzzle, the next logical step is to put them together to create the outside border. This is not just my next easy win, but a step that clearly establishes the boundaries of my work-in-progress. It creates a frame that begins to reveal where the many additional pieces might fit according to both shape and pattern. It coordinates and affirms placement and helps prevent misalignment of the inside pieces.

Framing also provides a sense of stability to the big picture and sets the boundaries that help to clarify what goes where. Used in this way boundaries are inclusionary, welcoming the pieces into the big picture, guiding proper placement, and creating an environment of belonging.

Looking back at the leadership program we were developing, the structure started to become clear during the planning process. We saw how certain lessons belonged together, and the content boundaries we created were based on the categorization of course modules, giving the program structure, and making it easier to decide what lesson topics should be included into which module.

As a leader, it is important that you establish project boundaries that emphasize what is included as well as what is restricted. Project boundaries may include things like budget, materials, time frames, and confidentiality.

> Establish project boundaries that emphasize what is included as well as what is restricted.

It is also important to understand and respect the boundaries of your individual team members. Team and individual boundaries may include things like qualifications, essential functions, work hours, quotas, time off, responsibilities, and security access.

Disregarding or minimizing boundaries can break apart the framing that is meant to both let in and hold things together. This puts your team and the big picture at risk.

Here are some typical boundary breakers:

- Sending an email to team members after working hours: You want to get the message out as soon as you think of it, and sometimes that is after hours. But getting it off your plate can unintentionally cause stress and set an expectation for your employees to act upon it immediately. However, most email programs have a setting that allows you to set a date and time when your message will be sent. Use this setting to send your message the next business day. This way you can write your email after hours when it is fresh in your mind, and the system will hold it in the outbox until the date and time you set for delivery.

- Micromanaging break time: Respecting a team member's earned break time during a busy day recognizes the value of the team member as more than just a means to an end. If your team members are hesitant to take their breaks for fear of being questioned (or timed), overall team morale will suffer. Instead, be a leader who recognizes how important breaks are and encourage your team members to take break time to clear their heads, rest their eyes, step away and shake the tension out of their bodies, and return to their work areas ready to re-engage.

- Relying too much on the "Other Duties as Assigned": Often written into job descriptions, this statement makes it too easy for leaders to overstep the boundaries of a person's role and responsibilities and can have negative effects on both morale and productivity.

What Does This Teach Us about Leadership?

While framing is important for project assignments, goals, and time management, it is also an important part of clarifying and respecting a team member's role and responsibilities. By taking the time to review and discuss position descriptions and the essential functions that define and frame the context of duties that fall within each job description, leaders help team members understand how

> Understand and respect the boundaries of your individual team members.

assignments connect their roles within the bigger picture and allows them to set reasonable boundaries, giving them some control over their workloads. The result is empowered and productive team members who better manage their tasks and avoid burnout.

In her book, *Humanity Works Better*, author Debbie Cohen shares,

> *"Boundaries are there to let people in – not keep people out. Boundaries, at their best, establish clear guidelines around behaviors that create a sense of safety and wellbeing and are essential for forming authentic trust."* [4]

Wellness Perspective

During the pandemic, many people I talked to discovered that their work seemed to be taking longer, meetings were more frequent, and overall workload was increasing. Efforts of those who attempted to retain normal work hours were thwarted by messages at all hours of a day, including weekends, bombarded by emergent assignments with short timelines for completion, and long workdays with very few breaks.

Lack of boundaries created an "always-on" culture. Some of this arises from people not being clear on what is expected of them, some from people in leadership positions expressing concern about whether people are actually working despite the long hours and increased workloads, and some from people feeling unable to set boundaries in the way they were pre-pandemic.

With many organizations still embracing remote and hybrid models of work, stated boundaries for workdays, projects, and communication parameters are necessary, or risk of burnout and illness increase. Fatigue due to excessive work and uncertainty threaten the health and well-being of all team members.

Experimentation with work schedules that include core hours while allowing for flexibility during the workday helps reduce stress for team members who are juggling multiple responsibilities. Further, having the opportunity to work at home has enabled many people to learn about and maximize their own productive times of day. People who can avoid the daily commute will add more productive time to their day, and many colleagues report appreciating the additional time to tend to healthy activities, which increases their mental and physical energy. According to Gallup, overall, organizations that adopt flexible work arrangements have experienced a stronger sense of commitment and engagement by their workforce. [5]

Challenge: Establish Guidelines

Look at either a project you have recently assigned, or one you plan to assign.

1. Create a project info sheet that clearly identifies the project boundaries as applicable (such as budget, materials, time frames, confidentiality, authorization levels, etc.).
2. Make a list of the positions (not the people) that report to you.
   a. Review the position descriptions. Do they create accurate and realistic frames that properly align the tasks and assignments with the role and its responsibilities?
   b. Do your expectations for the roles fall within their frames?
3. People apply for positions based on job descriptions. When they search for a job, they look for postings that align with their knowledge, skills, abilities, and availability. When they see a potential fit for them, it is based on how the job is framed.
   a. How much do you rely on the Other Duties as Assigned to justify what you require of those positions (and the people in them)?
   b. Take some time to recalibrate expectations to properly align with the essential functions and responsibilities of your team members' official roles and responsibilities.

Organize and Assess

Get to Know the Puzzle Pieces

Once I have my frame done (well 99 percent of it because there are always a few edges I have not found yet that my eye will catch eventually, and that is OK!), it is time to get a sense of the rest of the puzzle challenge. I spread out the remaining pieces, face up on a flat surface, and take some time to observe their shapes, colors, and patterns. This helps me more easily find the right fit when I'm working through the sections. Some pieces show me clearly where they belong in the big picture, and others have characteristics that blend in and are more difficult to place. Then there are the uniquely shaped pieces that I set aside for those moments when the other pieces that come together create the perfect spaces for their unique contributions.

Organizing can also take on different approaches, depending on where I am in the puzzle building process. I often begin by laying them all out randomly so I can scan across them to see what stands out. Other times I might take the time to cluster them together by image likeness so I can see the subtle variances. Then as I get closer to puzzle completion, I might decide it will be easier to find the ones I need if I rearrange them by shape since the more the puzzle comes together, the easier it is to see the missing shapes needed for a particular space.

What Does This Teach Us about Leadership?

As a leader, it is important to recognize the ways that each team member fits into the big picture of your organization. It is important to take in a wide view of the entire team so you can see how each one stands out in their own way, then take the time to get to know the unique technical and interpersonal skills of each individual and understand what motivates them so when you have to fill a specific project need, you can easily see which team members would be a good fit.

In addition to knowing and trusting their people, leaders must also know themselves. A leader's strengths (and limitations) can be used as building blocks for creating a culture of interdependence and trust within a team. Self-awareness is both a leadership vulnerability and an often-untapped superpower.

John Maxwell, an internationally recognized leadership expert, speaker, and author tells us,

> *"Team leaders have to connect with their team and themselves. If they don't know their team's strengths and weaknesses, they cannot hand off responsibilities to the team."* [6]

At one point in the course development process my leadership program team struggled with some content topics that were more challenging to place. Some of the topic lessons we chose to include could easily belong in more than one module, so we had to look at each one in order to strategically decide the best placement. This process would ensure a smoother learning path for the end user. Once it was decided where and how the topics

> In addition to knowing and trusting their people, leaders must also know themselves.

would work best in the course modules, assigning them to the appropriate team was the next step.

Whether they are puzzle pieces, project pieces, or people, leaders need to see them, know their strengths, and position them for success within the overall vision of the organization.

Wellness Perspective

We all know how we feel when we are accepted and appreciated for who we are and what we bring to our workplace; being valued is extremely rewarding and creates a desire to make more, and greater, contributions to the organization. In his book, *Strengths Finder 2.0*, Tom Rath states,

> *"People who have the opportunity to focus on their strengths every day are six times as likely to be engaged in their jobs and more than three times as likely to report having an excellent quality of life in general."* [7]

A neuroscience study concluded that,

> *"[R]ecognition has the largest effect on trust when it occurs immediately after a goal has been met, when it comes from peers, and when it's tangible, unexpected, personal, and public."* [8]

When leaders recognize team members for their contribution, skills, and attributes, a stronger and more trusting relationship is formed, which can lead to greater willingness to become involved in projects, as well as reinforce the importance and richness of a diverse workplace.

Challenge: Organize It

1. Take some time to identify each team member's strengths (talent, skill, knowledge, attribute, and interest). These may be things you see in them, or you can ask them to tell you what strengths they see in themselves. Keep in mind that strengths can come in a variety of forms.

   Here are some examples:

   - Detail oriented
   - Patient
   - Social
   - Adaptable
   - Creative
   - Analytical
   - Facilitator
   - Logical
   - Optimistic
   - Supportive
   - Technologically savvy
   - Problem solver
   - Persuasive
   - Empathetic
   - Good communicator
   - Collaborative
   - Researcher
   - Quick learner

2. How do your team members' strengths both complement and support each other in meeting the goals and expectations of your department? Share these thoughts with your team.
3. Are there any competing strengths among them that need to be coached toward collaboration rather than competition in order to maintain a productive work environment?
4. Be aware of and share a list of professional development offerings and actively accommodate these opportunities for your team members to affirm and take their strengths to the next level.

All too often leaders recommend training courses only to address team member weaknesses and/or behavioral issues. While there are circumstances where training for skill remediation is necessary, it is just as important to provide strengths-based training opportunities to build a work culture where potential is recognized, and individual strengths are rewarded rather than taken for granted.

Milestones Matter

A Milestone Is a Goal within the Larger Goal

For example, the big picture goal is the completed puzzle. My first major milestone is having my outside border completed. As I continue, I will set additional milestones for the sections of the puzzle that I hope to focus on next. I may even plan out potential milestones before I start. If I have someone working on the puzzle with me, we might work together to find and place the pieces for a particular section, or we might each focus on a different section, working on two milestones at the same time. Every milestone brings us closer to completing the puzzle, and as I see the puzzle picture emerging, I get motivated to keep going.

Milestones organize and affirm our progress and measure our success. They break down the big picture into manageable parts and hold us accountable for the part we play in moving things forward. Establishing milestones frees us to zoom in on the details of the individual parts of the whole. Some are easy wins, and some are more challenging. Seeing the results of our efforts is satisfying, especially when we get through a particularly difficult part.

In a study reported by *Forbes*, researchers identified what they called the Progress Principle,

"[T]he single most important thing during a workday is making progress in meaningful work. ... [T]he more often they experience that sense of progress, the more likely they will be productive." [9]

The concept of milestones is entrenched in our human development. Whether it is taking our first steps, celebrating birthdays and graduations, or getting a driver's license or first job, we measure our lives in milestones that matter to us. Making meaning of our lives and our work is what keeps us going and makes it all worthwhile.

> Milestones hold us accountable for the part we play in moving things forward.

What Does This Teach Us about Leadership?

As a leader, it is important to both help establish and recognize the achievement of milestones within a project. It also helps you organize how you will delegate the parts of the whole. This keeps you connected to the project and the people who will make things happen.

But in order to be effective, milestones need to have reasonable expectations to support appropriate levels of motivation and engagement. They need to represent specific accomplishments within the overall goal, ones that a team member can see themselves achieving. Having a specific time frame for planned completion is also a key component.

One of the milestones for our leadership program was to schedule one-on-one interviews with members of the executive team to record their personal stories about how they model leadership in their roles. Topics included trust, work-life harmony, composure, team building, and conflict resolution to name a few. Completing the scheduling, recording, and editing of the videos was celebrated as a major milestone accomplishment and an important piece of the course vision coming to life for the team.

Wellness Perspective

When setting timelines for milestones, it is important to acknowledge what can realistically be accomplished with the time and energy available to devote to a project. Milestones frame a project with achievable goals, enabling your team to experience the rewarding sense of accomplishment while staying aware of how much still needs to be done. Achieving a milestone requires discipline because so many competing priorities threaten progress. So, when these short-term goals are attained, the feeling of self-efficacy gets another boost, along with the sense of confidence in the ability to persevere and produce something worthwhile. Albert Bandura, a social psychologist explains that,

> *"Self-efficacy is a person's belief in their ability to complete a task or achieve a goal. It encompasses a person's confidence in themselves to control their behavior, exert an influence over their environment, and stay motivated in pursuit of their goal."* [10]

Celebrating milestones can strengthen personal relationships and commitment to the work. Calling attention to successes can generate collective energy to see the project through to completion. Every time a milestone is reached, the exhilaration is a great reminder of how being personally invested in the work and having strong relationships with colleagues contributes to our well-being.

When leaders ensure that each milestone is celebrated in some way, it becomes further validation of everyone's contribution to a project, and what a diverse team can do when pooling their strengths. Even small acknowledgments by people in leadership positions can fuel the energy to persist through challenges and see a project through to completion.

Challenge: Milestones Matter

Project management is all about milestones and timelines. Milestones are the individual pieces that need to come together for progress, and timelines set the expectations for efficiency. They should be aligned, coordinated, and manageable by the team.

1. Goal assessment – Choose a recent project and organize it into milestones and timelines. What milestones can be done at the same time, and which ones rely on the completion of other milestones prior to starting?
2. What external dependencies can impact progress and efficiency (materials, budget, technology, other departments, other project deadlines, etc.)?
3. Discuss your assessment of the goal with your team to get their input.

Part Two

LEADERSHIP

Diversity

Diversity is all around us. In the workplace setting, diversity can include racial, religious, cultural, gender, age, sexual orientation, gender diversity, and different disabilities. Your employees can live in different neighborhoods, drive different vehicles, have different hairstyles, buy different products, participate in different activities, listen to different music, follow different traditions, and eat different foods.

These same employees bring an important mix of interests, skills, perspectives, and talents into our work environments. These human differences provide us with opportunities for greater understanding and invitations to discover new ways of thinking, being, and doing.

Diversity is also critical for establishing an environment of variety and balance that can thrive within a culture of support and interconnection.

Included in Part Two:

Diversity and Interconnection

Teamwork - It Might Take Two

All Are Unique and Important

Belonging and Connection

Diversity and Interconnection

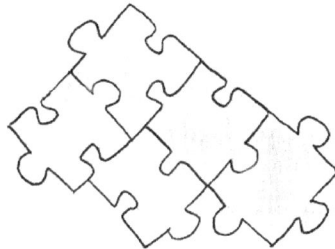

Diversity Helps Us Learn and Grow

I have been asked if I have ever done a jigsaw puzzle using only the back of the pieces, or completed a puzzle that is all one color.

While some may be up for that level of challenge, the big picture is what matters to me. It is the one that contains a diversity of color and shapes coming together in shared connectivity that makes the puzzle-building process and outcome enjoyable for me.

While there is still diversity within the puzzle shapes if I flip all the pieces over, other than the added challenge of doing it that way, I do not want to make something more difficult than it should be.

The diversity in a jigsaw puzzle is most often seen in the physical and most obvious aspects of shape, color, and pattern. But when we look deeper, diversity is also found in the process and the people who are working on it. Diversity can also include the formative influences and experiences of those participating.

Take the example of a puzzle I did with someone that included a collage of different brands and logos. The pieces that were easier for me to find and place belonged to the products with which I was familiar. I grew up with these logos, so they stood out for me immediately in the scattered pieces. The other brands were more difficult for me to find, but they were easier for the person who is from another geographic area where those products were the more familiar brands for them. It made for great conversation and reminded me of the value that our historical diversity of experiences brings to a project. Diversity makes puzzles, life, and workplace collaboration more interesting!

Avoid a Group Think Culture

Think about how great it would be to see your team members quickly reach agreement on a plan or decision. Now think about how that might mean something is missing. Respectful debate and disagreement within a group discussion is a sign of a psychologically safe team culture based on trust. The absence of it may be a sign of your team falling into what is known as group think.

Group think is something that happens when everyone on the team simply jumps to agreement with the first idea or decision offered so they don't have to spend any more time with it and can get back to the other things they are doing. It is the easy path forward. Group think can be a symptom of many things including no clear connection to the decision being made, not feeling psychologically safe to speak up in disagreement, an already overloaded schedule, a lack of understanding, a need to impress the boss, and peer pressure to name a few. All these things can cause self-censorship in team members which sabotages creativity and forward thinking.

During a team meeting, I noticed how an employee with a strong personality quickly swayed the other team members with ideas for a new training program without any further contributions from the group. Rather than engage with this individual and provide alternative ideas for the program, the team just followed that person's lead and nodded in agreement to the recommendations. Witnessing what was happening, I quickly joined the conversation by affirming the idea as a good start for a Plan A. Then I challenged the other team members to come up with additional ideas since it is always a good practice to have a Plan B, and a Plan C. Once new ideas were shared, I voiced my appreciation for all three plans and the team went on to discuss the pros and cons of each one. While

> Respectful debate and disagreement within a group discussion is a sign of a psychologically safe team culture based on trust.

the team did end up deciding to go with Plan A, some of the ideas from the backup plans made their way into it and all team members became more openly engaged in the planning.

What Does This Teach Us about Leadership?

Somewhere beyond where nobody speaks up and everybody agrees is a place where true innovation thrives. This is a place where team members feel comfortable sharing and exploring different ideas, perspectives, and experiences that stimulate deeper discussion, healthy debate, critical reasoning, evaluation of consequences, and collaborative decision-making. This place is created by leaders who value diversity in all its forms and who find ways to make room for what all team members bring to the table.

We all need to explore the many forms of diversity and recognize how it enriches our lived experience when embraced.

Wellness Perspective

We interact with people different from ourselves on a daily basis, and it is important to value these differences as being enriching to our lives. We realize from our interactions with others that learning is not always knowing more; sometimes it is knowing differently. A sense of well-being can result from realizing that we have grown personally and professionally by gaining a wide range of insightful perspectives.

Ranstad, the world's largest talent company shares,

> *"Employees from diverse backgrounds have different perspectives and points of view thanks to their culture and education. When working together on a project, they bring their own frame of mind and are able to challenge each other, which allows for unique and varied ideas to emerge. Team creativity is stimulated and the capacity for innovation is strengthened."* [11]

Consider a time when you worked with people having close to the same characteristics as yourself: age, cultural heritage, socioeconomic status, etc. The environment was likely quite comfortable. Then someone with a different ethnicity, generation, or any other trait joined your workplace, and discomfort arose over not knowing how to act or speak around this new person. If the person becomes marginalized and is not accepted, the individual's health and well-being are affected, and the team loses an opportunity to gain valuable insights from this person.

As a leader, remember that you are always "on" for your team. The behaviors and attitudes you model about the many forms of diversity set the stage for your team's cohesion and ultimate performance.

Challenge: Diversity

1. Managing and capitalizing on the many forms of diversity that your team brings to the table is an important role for leadership.
    a. Recognize and value the important role that diversity plays in team building and innovation.

   b. Talk to your team about how their formative influences help bring diverse perspectives to their collaborative work.

   c. Show your appreciation for the unique skills and talents that make your team innovative and productive.

2. Talk about the concept of group think with your team.

   a. Discuss how to create an environment of psychological safety where all contributions are respected.

Teamwork
It Might Take Two

Look Again...

Once, I spent a long time looking for a specific piece. I even took breaks hoping that when I returned it would jump out at me as had happened so many times before, but it just was not happening. I was looking for a shape that was a perfect fit and it was nowhere to be found.

That is when I realized that maybe it would take two pieces to fill this space. It turned out that this was, in fact, the case. Once I shifted my perception of what I needed to accomplish my task, I was able to locate the two pieces and successfully fill in the empty space.

As leaders, we often look for the team member who can complete the picture for us (whatever that picture may be on any given day). Sometimes we find what we are looking for, but often the exact blend of skills and abilities in one person is hard to find. This is an example of how we might default an important assignment to a star performer, when, in fact, they may not possess all the required knowledge and skills on their own to be the right fit.

What Does This Teach Us about Leadership?

When a leader has taken the time to know their team member's strengths and interests, they can easily pair up dynamic teams of two or three who will blend their skill sets to meet the challenges together and get things done. An additional benefit is that you are assigning, empowering, and initiating knowledge sharing while moving efficiently toward the end goal. By working together with complementary and interdependent skill sets, team members create interpersonal bonds and build trusting relationships that do not often happen when everyone is always focusing on their own thing.

But I get it. We don't want to put more resources into a project than is necessary. That includes our people. Why put two people on one task when they could each be working on getting two things done at once? On the surface, this makes sense. When you see it only from that perspective, you easily see more things "making progress." This was what I thought until a member of my team started coming to me for help more often than usual. Every day there were more questions and I picked up on an increase in stress and a drop in confidence. I initiated a check-in to address my observation. It turned out that while they were making good progress on most things, there were some tasks within the overall assignment that they simply were not sure how to do. This is an example of how a paired team with a complementary set of skills would be a better option. So, I paired them up with a coworker who was strong in the required skill set and together they worked on each other's projects, each contributing their strengths to the tasks at hand.

> By working together with complementary and interdependent skill sets, team members create interpersonal bonds and build trusting relationships.

Combining their skills kept both projects moving forward and initiated a learning opportunity for both that paid off in the long run.

Evan Leybourne of the Business Agility Institute shares,

> *"One of the key qualitative advantages of pair work, is the implicit skills and knowledge transfer between partners. This includes both specific skills relating directly to the task, and general knowledge transfer relating to work techniques and expertise."* [12]

So next time that you have a work assignment, rather than just looking for the team member who is a perfect match for an assignment, it is important to be open to the possibility that a better fit might be two or three team members working together, each contributing their share of the necessary skills and abilities for a successful outcome!

Wellness Perspective

Matching team members with complementary strengths can expedite a project with increased efficiency. This approach can validate a feeling of being appreciated for both competencies and contribution. Further, pairing diverse team members can lead to mutual understanding and appreciation for differences as well as finding commonalities. Sharing the workload can foster inclusion through personal connection and shared goals.

A team member who enjoys data entry and is adept in routine processes who is paired with one who is more conceptually oriented can enable both to remain mentally engaged and motivated to complete a project together, which provides an opportunity for each person to learn from one another and expand their competencies.

Self-Determination Theory tells us that at times when many people are expressing dissatisfaction with their workplace, personal connection can be a factor in promoting a sense of belonging, and can also create a feeling of autonomy, which is empowering and rewarding for team members at all levels within an organization.[13]

Challenge: It Might Take Two

1. Think about a recent project or task where you chose a specific person to work on a specific goal.
   a. How did you choose that person? What skills and abilities were you searching for?
   b. Could this person have been paired up with another team member where their combined strengths could have improved the outcome or shortened the timeline?
2. For the next project or task, choose two team members whose combined individual skills strengthen the potential for success.
   a. What additional benefits can be gained by pairing up team members for tasks?

All Are Unique and Important

Create a Palate for Success

While management is about the *how* (ways of moving forward toward a goal), leadership is about the *who* (motivating, inspiring, and supporting the pieces that get us there). This is where we look again at the individual pieces that bring the big picture to life.

When puzzling, I try to avoid the individual pieces getting lost, chewed up, or bent out of shape. If one gets lost, my puzzle will never be complete. If one gets knocked onto the floor and ends up as a dog snack, it will be damaged to the point of not fitting in the space where it belongs. If I do not handle each piece carefully, it might get bent out of shape and the connections with other pieces will suffer.

What Does This Teach Us about Leadership?

As leaders, it is important to recognize and celebrate the unique skills and abilities of our team members. The strengths-based approach to managing means focusing on individual strengths and nurturing a team whose members' strengths complement rather than compete with one another. It is also about recognizing and respecting the individual ways they prefer to be coached, supported, and recognized. An article in Glass Door for Employers shares this advice,

> *"[H]umans are wired to think independently and desire a certain amount of individual affirmation and recognition for their specific work outside of the team. Enabling employees to own their individual value in a teamwork environment is not only empowering for the individual but energizing for the company as a whole."* [14]

Should a piece of a puzzle get bent out of shape, I carefully work to get it back to its original form. I do not ignore it or push it aside, because it is needed to complete the big picture. The same is true with your team members. They may get bent out of shape now and then, and it is up to you to help them by addressing the issues at hand and not ignoring them. Maybe it is a team conflict that you need to help resolve or a need for encouragement to move beyond mistakes made. By showing up with curiosity, respect, and genuine care for your team members you will be doing your part in helping to keep them engaged, connected, and productive.

I experienced this when a member of my team resigned to pursue a new career opportunity. Another team member applied for the position and when the hiring committee made their recommendation, this employee was in the top three but not the chosen candidate. While I agreed with this decision, it was not an easy conversation to have. I understood the hurt and disappointment (in this case this employee was the "bent out of shape" puzzle piece), but as they got to know the new hire, they began to understand why I had made that decision. Throughout this process, I encouraged engagement with the new hire and reaffirmed the employee's value to the team. After taking the time needed emotionally and mentally, the employee came back to being fully engaged.

Wellness Perspective

Being treated with respect maintains people's dignity and lets them know they are valued as individuals and for what they bring to the team. A workplace that emphasizes mutual respect as a cultural norm promotes empathy and helps to reduce the effect of stressors. When we feel respected, we're more confident in sharing ideas, which leads to higher creativity and fosters innovation.

In a team environment, each person is integral to the project. Working cooperatively ensures that each person is heard and can demonstrate their knowledge and skills *and* be acknowledged for their contribution.

Just as pieces need one another to complete the puzzle, we benefit from the connection with others as we pool our strengths. The feeling of fulfillment we get when we are respected and can contribute to the success of a project is a strong contributor to well-being and career satisfaction.

When a leader delegates a task or role that is considered a "stretch goal," this is an indicator of confidence in the team member, and an opportunity to diversify skills and abilities. Employees rise to challenge, lead-

> Employees who feel respected are more confident in sharing ideas, which leads to higher creativity and fosters innovation.

ing them to become better versions of themselves. This is empowering and rewarding, a major boost to their personal, professional, and social well-being!

Challenge: All Are Unique and Important

1. Reflect on your team members from a strengths-based approach and write down the strengths that come to mind.
   a. How do their strengths complement the strengths of their teammates?
   b. Are there competing strengths? How can you turn competition into collaboration?
   c. Sometimes team members do not recognize, or they minimize their strengths. Spend time during reviews and check-ins to affirm and discuss these strengths and discuss ways to further build upon them.
2. When you consider how you take care of your team members, what ways come to mind?
   a. Talk with your team members about what came to mind for you and what they feel they need from you in order to feel like you have their best interests at heart. This requires a commitment to supporting a culture of psychological safety.
   b. Reflect on your approach to resolving conflicts. If your tendency is to be disciplinary, try switching your approach to one of respect, curiosity, and problem solving. Conflict is a symptom; explore for the cause and work on that.
   c. Check team member bandwidth: is there something going on that is causing a distraction?
      i. Emotional - grief, stress, frustration, insecurity.
      ii. Situational - schedule change, moving households, sudden increase in personal responsibilities.
      iii. Physical - exhaustion, illness, pain.
      iv. Developmental/Intellectual - lack of understanding, need for additional training, coaching, or mentoring.

Belonging and Connection

Emphasize Purpose and Interdependence

Belonging and connection means that the qualities each piece offers are needed, will be a good fit, and their contributions will help ensure a successful outcome.

As I search for a specific piece to place, I look at the qualities each piece has to offer. I look for characteristics that support appropriate placement into the big picture. Sometimes I find a piece that almost fits, and I find myself pushing on it a bit too hard because I want it to be the right piece when it is not. I cannot make it fit just because I want it to.

I once found a piece that was a perfect fit for shape, but the pattern was off. It still belonged. It just belonged in another part of the big picture, so I used its shape as a guide. It may not have been the right piece for that space, but it helped me find what I was looking for, and I eventually found its rightful place in another section. I need to remember that I cannot force things. Instead, I need to be patient and find the right fit for each piece, and the right piece for each fit.

For a jigsaw puzzle, the big picture is the environment in which each separate piece both belongs and connects with the others.

Belonging and connection are important. A McKinsey & Company article emphasizes this point stating,

> *"To retain employees, organizations need to evolve their approach to building community, cohesion, and a sense of belonging at work. ... Employees want stronger relationships, a sense of connection, and to be seen."* [15]

Once when I was assigning team members to a project work group, I made the mistake of placing someone who was not really a good fit for a particular group. This person was enthusiastic, a great team player, and a people-person but the technical experience this group assignment relied on was not a strength. This slowed the team's progress and as a result, the team struggled to keep things moving forward. Recognizing this was a valued and successful member of my team, I realized this was a failure on my part to put them in the right group for their skill set. I resolved this by reassigning the more technical responsibilities associated with the project and changing their focus to the outreach and marketing involved for the program launch. The employee flourished in this role and the rest of the team was back to performing as a highly functional and productive team.

When what team members have to offer is in alignment with the expectations of a particular environment, they thrive together, and projects unfold as they should. Each piece belongs somewhere and connects to something. It is the leader's job to make sure that when projects are assigned, competencies align with the needs and expectations of the big picture.

What Does This Teach Us about Leadership?

As leaders, we need to make sure that we are not just looking for the skills needed (like the shape of my puzzle piece), but also a fit within the culture (like the pattern of my puzzle piece). When assigning team members to tasks and projects, placing someone who is a good fit in attitude and interpersonal skills is just as critical to success as are the technical skills and knowledge that the team member brings.

I also want to make sure that the pieces in the puzzle box actually belong to the puzzle I am working on.

If there are pieces in the mix that belong to another puzzle, they will end up getting overlooked and left out instead of being valued and needed. They still have valuable things to offer, just not in this particular puzzle. Somewhere there is another puzzle looking for exactly what they offer: an environment that cannot be complete without them. Leaders need to be able to both recognize and support where their team members belong within the big picture of their department's active projects.

> Placing someone who is a good fit in attitude and interpersonal skills is just as critical to success as are the technical skills and knowledge that the team member brings.

Wellness Perspective

A sense of belonging is essential to our mental health. The social connection that contributes to belonging is valuable to our self-worth.

We also know the satisfaction and connection of feeling like we fit in. We feel less stressed and on edge and are more likely to express ourselves without fear of being judged or rejected. During the pandemic, when people were disconnected physically from one another, many said they stayed in contact virtually and spent a significant amount of time reminiscing about times when they were together. It was a way to keep the ties strong and to validate each person's feeling of still belonging to a group. In fact, many colleagues stated that their relationships were made stronger, because they realized how important the people in their lives were.

Some pointed out that acquaintances became friends, and that this was immensely gratifying.

In the workplace, a shared sense of purpose and acknowledgment of each person's contribution promotes a sense of belonging to a team. The US Surgeon General's Framework takes belonging a step further and emphasizes the well-being value of "mattering" at work:

> *"People want to know that they matter to those around them and that their work matters. Knowing you matter has been shown to lower stress, while feeling you do not can increase the risk for depression."* [16]

The Surgeon General's Framework for Workplace Well-Being and Mental Health has five areas of focus that include: Protect from Harm, Connection and Community, Work/Life Harmony, Mattering at Work, and Opportunity for Growth.

It further states that,

> *"Prosocial behavior promotes positive social relationships through welcoming, helping, and reassuring others. Organizational cultures that promote belonging can also foster a powerful protective force against bias, discrimination, and exclusion in the workplace. Organizational leaders should cultivate environments and cultures where connection is encouraged, and workers of all backgrounds are included."* [17]

We all contribute to shaping our workplace culture, through the ways we express and exemplify our values, the way we treat others, and the integrity we possess. In turn, we are shaped by our environment. This reciprocity can be a key factor in creating a culture of well-being for all.

Challenge: Belonging and Connection

1. Write a description of your workplace culture. Then discuss the following with your team:
   a. How does it measure up to the five areas of the Surgeon General's framework?
      i. In what areas can you better align your environment with the framework?
      ii. What values, expectations, and attitudes support belonging and connection in the workplace?
2. Team cohesion is critical to productivity and team morale. Write down two ways you can help develop team cohesion at work.
3. Review how you respond to mistakes made or work not progressing.
   Try this next time:
   a. Rather than reassigning the failed tasks to someone else, try encouraging and supporting the team member in trying again. Find ways to help them succeed.
      i. Did they fully understand the process?
      ii. Did they try a different approach? (Appreciate the effort and discuss next attempt.)
      iii. Did they have access to the resources and information they needed?
      iv. Might this be a "it might take two" lesson for you?
4. Plan and schedule a non-work retreat. Do something fun or challenging together at least once a year (preferably twice a year) that is not work related. This emphasizes that yes, the work is important but so are team member dynamics and well-being.

Part Three

When moving toward a shared vision, workplace culture is the social operating system that defines how we treat each other and how we get things done. Everything that happens in the day-to-day falls into one of those two categories.

Workplace culture starts with the common purpose, the vision and mission of the organization. It then flows through the company's policies, goals, expectations, and work environment into the employee experience. From there, it makes its way to the customer experience.

Included in Part Three:

Some Things Just Take Time

Saturation Prevents Progress

The Value of Taking Breaks

Choose a Different Approach

Process Can Inhibit Progress

Fail Fast – Fail Forward

Some Things Just Take Time

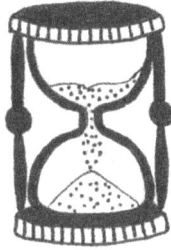

Don't Rush It

There is no getting around it. Jigsaw puzzles take time, and some require more than others. Completion time is based on the complexity of the puzzle, the number of and shapes of the pieces, the image and color patterns, how many people are working on it, and the resources available to sort and lay out the pieces. It is unreasonable to require quicker completion because the next one you ordered was just delivered to your doorstep!

When I start a new puzzle, I use my dining room table as a surface for putting it together. I also have two cardboard panels on which I sort and lay out my pieces. Whenever I take a break or am done for the day, I simply stack these panels on top of the puzzle-in-progress. Under everyday circumstances, this process works well, and I can set a pace that is manageable within the context of my other daily responsibilities.

Now imagine that I have invited guests over for dinner. It would not make sense for me to start a new puzzle the day before this engagement and expect it to be done before then. Securing additional resources (a dedicated puzzle table, for example) would solve this issue and I would be able to start or continue to work on the puzzle anytime. However, if I do not have the budget, or the physical space available for one, I must work within the constraints I have and slow the start of my next puzzle project until after my dinner party (or cancel my dinner party).

I also need to recognize that some puzzles are more challenging and completing them will take longer and require me to be patient with the process. Finding the edge pieces takes time but is an important task that makes future progress easier. Flipping all the pieces onto the panels with the print side up might be a boring chore when I am anxious to start putting pieces together, but it becomes worth the time it takes when I need to scan for certain colors or patterns. Re-arranging pieces by shape is time consuming, but in the long run it helps me find the right pieces more quickly as my puzzle comes together. All these tasks take time. But each one is necessary and should not be rushed.

If I do not allow for the time it takes to do these things, the overall experience is impacted in ways that make the challenge more difficult, frustrating, and time consuming. Trying to rush through these tasks takes away from the enjoyment of doing the puzzle.

What Does This Teach Us about Leadership?

Too often leaders assign projects with narrow timelines and do not consider the steps and time required to complete them. This causes team members to feel pressured and rushed which only risks mistakes, injury, or low-quality outcomes, especially if resources are limited. As a leader, try to minimize giving assignments with an unreasonable timeline for completion, and when it is inevitable, recognize the impact on the stress levels of your team members, the projects and tasks being pushed aside, and on the quality impact of the rushed assignment.

Melissa Eisler, of Wide Lens Leadership writes,

"If you learn to slow down ... [y]ou will move faster toward your long-term goals and priorities. ...You will make fewer mistakes. You will communicate more clearly and make better decisions. Most importantly, as a leader, you will create a stronger and more productive and energizing team culture." [18]

Not every project needs to be committed to a firm deadline. Try setting "planned completion dates" instead of "goal deadlines" since it allows room for unexpected challenges, delays, and learning curves. Setting planned completion dates whenever possible eases pressure on the team should things happen that are out of their control and offers the added advantage of reducing team member stress by keeping focus on the process, not the ticking clock. This way when an urgent request is assigned that has a critical time-sensitive deadline, ongoing projects can be more easily prioritized, and the new project will get the additional time, resources, focus, and commitment it requires.

My team experienced a planned completion date delay when we needed to move our program's kickoff date from March to July due to outside factors. Even though it was a delay from the original timeline, it worked out better overall because the extra time allowed us to include all the course content we had in the original outline. Nothing had to be cut and managers were given more lead time to plan their availability to participate in the course.

> Setting "planned completion dates" allows room for unexpected challenges, delays, and learning curves.

Wellness Perspective

Too often, leaders assign a project with a short deadline without understanding the cascade effect on the team members who will need to complete the project. With workdays already filled with responsibilities, and often having a few unanticipated tasks arise, people on the receiving end of delegated projects may find themselves in a predicament: too much work and not enough time or multiple tasks designated as high priority. Further, they often feel uncomfortable about speaking up, are unable to find help because everyone is busy, and do not have the autonomy to change their work structure to complete the short-term project first. The result is often a feeling of high stress and when prolonged, burnout can occur.

As shown in the Yerkes-Dodson curve, both acute and chronic stress lead to the tipping point for fatigue, exhaustion, and anxiety which breaks down people's concentration, analytical ability, attention to detail, and communication. We know that autonomy is a major factor in team member satisfaction, and feeling stuck in a time- and labor-intensive job without ability to manage workflow and volume leads to disengagement and chronic stressors, which could affect every aspect of life when they manifest as back pain, tension headaches, or lowered immunity to illness.

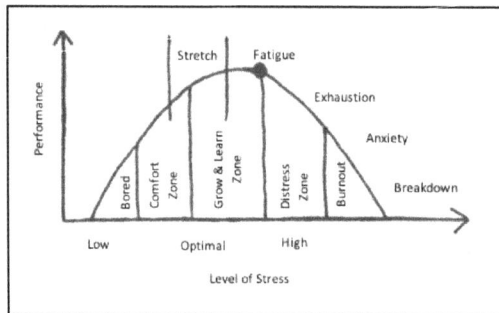

Source: Yerkes-Dodson Law: Inverted U-relationship between stress/arousal level and performance (see Teigen, 1994).[19]

Despite best efforts, a short-deadline project may arise. When this occurs, present a clearly defined path toward completion, and ensure that those tasked with the project have the knowledge, skills, and tools to execute the steps. Determining a project team and structure removes ambiguity and enables efficiency which keeps stress levels down.

Challenge: Some Things Just Take Time

1. Think of a recent task or project you assigned, or need to assign, with a next day or a short-term urgent deadline.
    a. Do you know the other tasks or assignments being worked on that have to be delayed because of your urgent request?
    b. What was/is the potential impact on the team member and their existing workload?
2. How can you reduce the number of urgent requests you ask of your team member?
3. What resources would help support these urgent requests?

Saturation Prevents Progress

Pay Attention to Bandwidth

While working on a puzzle one day, I knocked a glass of water onto my work area. A few of the puzzle pieces became saturated despite my attempts to minimize the damage from the spill. As the little cardboard pieces began to expand and the layers started curling up, I realized that these saturated pieces would no longer fit into the spaces where they belonged. Put simply, they would not be able to get their job done. So, I stopped what I was doing and took care of them by squeezing the water out and flattening them back into shape. Then I set them aside and gave them time to dry.

What Does This Teach Us about Leadership?

As leaders, it is important to avoid the tendency to default our requests to our star performers every time a new project comes along. How often do we go to the same people because of their proven track records of success before giving the task or opportunity to someone else who is just as qualified to take on the project or role?

In my career, I have seen this happen all too often and have on many occasions reminded leaders to give an opportunity to someone else when the same names kept being recommended for upcoming projects, committees, task forces, and search teams. The easy choices are not always the best choice if leaders want to build strong and

> How often do we default tasks to the same people before giving an opportunity to someone else who is just as qualified?

resilient teams whose members share responsibility and accountability.

Saturating a team member with an overload of responsibilities will ultimately end up in burnout, so it is important to be mindful of what you put on your team member's plate. They are rarely going to say it is too much for them to handle.

An article from Timely, reminds us,

> *"Workers want to impress and don't always feel capable of showing their vulnerability in case it leads to a missed promotion or poor performance review. Many put on a brave face and mask their excessive workloads."* [20]

Wellness Perspective

Much of the current literature on burnout provides tips for individuals on managing time, setting boundaries, taking breaks, getting enough sleep and, by the way, making sure to exercise and eat fresh, healthy food. But what about when people are not able to manage their own time at work, take breaks when they want, or establish their own boundaries on work responsibilities?

The stress of excessive workloads, along with the lack of autonomy in managing work, can lead to fatigue and frustration, and may decrease the ability to accomplish even small tasks effectively. When a leader is unaware of the amount of time and effort needed for projects, it becomes easy to delegate and see the work as just a little checklist, particularly when delegating to a star performer.

The word *just* is a minimizer. When attached to delegated work, the word *just* means it purportedly is an easily accomplished task, requiring minimal time and attention, when in reality the task may not be *just* one simple task, it may require many other elements and be quite detailed and involve communicating with others, looking up documents, accessing software systems, and checking calendars.

When team members have workloads with too many tasks, combined with inadequate support from coworkers and their leadership, the path to oversaturation and burnout becomes clearer. Further, a star performer has the added pressure of their reputation to uphold and may spend inordinate amounts of time during evenings or weekends trying to live up to the performance expectations.

In 2019, burnout was declared an occupational phenomenon by the World Health Organization: "a state of physical or emotional exhaustion that also involves a sense of reduced accomplishment and loss of personal identity." Dr. Christina Maslach from University of California, Berkeley, defined six factors that contribute to burnout: [21]

1. Unsustainable workload
2. Lack of control
3. Insufficient rewards for effort
4. Lack of supportive community
5. Lack of fairness
6. Mismatched values and skills

Even when people have relatively healthy personal habits, the organizational drivers of burnout can override their lifestyle actions. Leaders at all levels must remain aware of the ways a workplace environment contributes to work performance, and address those "wet puzzle pieces" before they become insurmountable problems.

Challenge: Saturation Prevents Progress

1. Take the time to assess the projects you have given to your staff or team.
   a. Are there certain staff members to whom you tend to assign more work? Take some time and explore why. If unchecked, this practice sets up potential burnout for some and prevents growth for others.
2. What changes can you make to become the leader that balances projects and workloads in ways that prevent saturation and burnout of your typical go-to team members while supporting growth and development for the rest of your team?

The Value of Taking Breaks

Model and Encourage Downtime

Once I have started a puzzle I want to keep the momentum of getting the next piece in place, and then the next. Often, I catch myself pressing on without thinking about how much time has passed. I forget to take my lunch break, my eyes lose focus, the pieces start to blur together, and no matter how hard I try to find that piece I need, it is nowhere in sight.

I start worrying that it is missing, or that I accidentally pushed it over the side of the table and onto the floor where my dog found it to be a yummy treat! My mind starts to place blame! It must be the dog, and, if not the dog, then the fault is with the manufacturer who packaged an incomplete puzzle.

Frustrated and discouraged, I finally take a break. I find something else to do, get something to eat, or just relax and listen to some music. Eventually I wander back to the puzzle, and there, staring right at me, is the piece that I need! It is right there in plain sight, not a manufacturer's defect and not a dog treat!

In my career as a training developer and facilitator, tapping into the creative part of my brain has been critical for the creation of my programs and training activities. For me, taking breaks is a necessity since it is the only way that my brain can shut down to rest and release the mental bandwidth that frees up the space for my creative ideas to flow. It is most often when I stop the constant stream of thinking, planning, and doing that new ideas pop into my mind and I get a rush of creativity. Whether or not these ideas make it into my big picture, I am never disappointed. Stopping to do nothing may sound boring and unproductive to some, but boredom creates the perfect environment for the mind to wander into its most productive and creative realm.

What Does This Teach Us about Leadership?

What I learned is the value of taking breaks for overall productivity. As leaders, if we push our team members too hard, with long hours and little time for breaks, we are sabotaging and chipping away their ability to focus on the tasks at hand. Alternatively, whether they are in the office or working remotely, when they are given the autonomy to take breaks or step away any time they need to, we are rewarded by an overall increase in creativity, engagement, and productivity!

> Show your team that you recognize the importance of knowing when to just press pause.

While planning a collegewide event with my team, it became evident that they were on overload and just trying to push through to the finish line. I could sense their creativity waning. It was Friday and it had been an intense week of brainstorming for this event. At 3 p.m., I suggested—no, I insisted—that everyone stop what they were doing and go home to start their weekend early! The change in their mood was clear: they needed this! And when they returned to work on Monday, they were refreshed and ready to tackle the week ahead with new ideas and recharged enthusiasm. Small actions such as this show your team that you are invested in their well-being and that you recognize the importance of knowing when to just press pause.

Wellness Perspective

While the world of work has changed significantly due to the pandemic, the old ideas about work having to be done at a desk, in an office or cubicle, for a set period of time (the nine-to-five tradition), the reality is that we have all learned how, when, and where work can be performed and completed with more flexible constraints. When the pandemic hit and we first started working from our homes, many people reported feeling reluctant to leave their computers, for fear of being perceived by their supervisors as not working. The increased distress of the pandemic combined with long workdays with few or no breaks, created or exacerbated both physical and mental health conditions.

Conversely, taking regular breaks at work refreshes the brain, increasing the ability to concentrate and to think both analytically and creatively, and also lowers decision fatigue, which is when people are so mentally fatigued that they default to the easiest decision rather than think through their choices. This contributes to impulsive decisions at work. (Imagine you are interviewing for a position with a hiring committee experiencing decision fatigue, when sound decision-making is compromised.) Sometimes the mind becomes so overwhelmed that a person is unable to complete work and procrastination or avoidance sets in.

The Take Back the Lunch Break survey by Tork concluded with this finding,

> *"Taking breaks throughout the workday has benefits for both the employee and the organization, but many employees often neglect to take them. Skipping breaks can lead to faster burnout and higher stress levels. Employees stepping away from*

work for a few minutes increases their productivity,
job satisfaction, mental health and well-being, and
are overall more engaged in their work." [22]

As we strive for quality of life, every action taken during the day matters because both healthy and unhealthy behaviors add up over time and affect well-being and the ability to function. A break for a few minutes every hour, every day, or just when needed, has a major positive effect over time. Movement, a few deep breaths to relax the brain, and hydrating with water, keep the body and mind functioning.

Challenge: The Value of Taking Breaks

1. Have a conversation with your team members about the value of recognizing when it is time to take breaks.
    a. Work together to establish guidelines so that team members have the autonomy to decide when to take breaks. For example, discuss how to best handle coverage when a team member needs a break.
2. Encourage your team members to step away from their work for a short break whenever they feel overwhelmed, drained, or stuck on an issue or process.
    a. Refrain from asking them where they were during their absence.
    b. Trust them. Every time.
3. Have a conversation about the impact of breaks.
    a. On overall productivity
    b. On physical, mental, and emotional well-being
    c. Were there any negative consequences? If yes, how can they be avoided when taking needed breaks?

Choose a Different Approach

Find Ways to Enjoy the Challenge

One of the puzzles I worked on had an image of a cat looking at bird feeders through a window facing the backyard. I completed that one twice but by the second time, I was not as motivated by the small wins and the milestones of completing the cat image first. I usually like to finish what I start, so I decided to make it more interesting by approaching it differently. Instead of finishing the cat first, I challenged myself to build the puzzle around the cat! Because of my new twist, my motivation shifted, and I enjoyed framing it and finishing the cat as the final milestone!

Not every task or project is interesting, stimulating, or enjoyable. Sometimes you must just press on. Staying mindful of how the task is critical to the big picture and finding new ways to move through tasks that are necessary but repetitive and boring can help keep the momentum from slowing down to a crawl.

What Does This Teach Us about Leadership?

As leaders, it is important to focus on end goals, processes, timelines, and productivity. It is equally important to recognize the value of each task's place in creating the end result and to recognize that team members will accomplish more when there is room to create new ways to approach the work. No job can be enjoyable all the time, but when there are opportunities to bring enjoyment into the process, it can make a difference in both outcomes and team member satisfaction.

A *Harvard Business Review* article by organizational leadership expert Jaewon Yoon shares,

> *"Thinking about how seemingly unimportant work belongs to a set of tasks contributing to a broader goal could help employees see its true value."* [23]

Getting there is the charge. Giving them the freedom to decide how to get there is empowering to the team and reveals your level of trust in their ability to be successful.

> Team members will accomplish more when there is room to create new ways to approach the work.

I like to encourage my team to find ways to help make the not-so-fun parts of their work more enjoyable. For example, I share with them how I love developing and facilitating experiential learning sessions. How I get into the zone and the room comes alive around me is energizing and exhilarating. On the flip side, putting together annual reports on my programs, not so much. I understand that the need to report on things like attendance, projected outcomes, and impact is a necessity because the return on investment is what keeps our programs going. So, I embrace the process and do my best to be creative with the data and images that tell the story of what we do and why it matters. Writing reports may not be exhilarating, but once completed it is both affirming and fulfilling.

> Empowering the team reveals your level of trust in their ability to be successful.

Wellness Perspective

Sometimes while working on the less interesting or enjoyable steps in a process, telling ourselves that we are learning something or confirming our understanding can create a feeling of satisfaction. Enjoying the overall process makes the tedious tasks more tolerable and can help keep motivation up.

It also helps us develop patience. In our busy lives, we drive fast, fidget in the checkout lane, and become impatient if we are kept on hold for more than a minute or two. The state of being perpetually on high alert taxes our energy and is detrimental to our health. Using mindful practices that promote a state of calm will increase the ability to focus and provide the patience to work through what we consider drudgery.

Focusing on the process may also help to define more efficient ways to complete a task. Process improvement can cut down the time needed on tasks and keep the mind attuned to new ways of doing things. This lights up the reward center in the brain and makes each task feel more meaningful. This is another way that mindfulness contributes to well-being.

When a project or activity is repetitive or boring, the tendency to attempt multitasking becomes stronger. The brain does not effect-tively focus on more than one task at a time. Instead, attention toggles between the activities a person is trying to perform concur-rently. This leads to reduced attention span, increased errors, and decreased accuracy, as well as a heightened sense of irritability and impatience.

One way to minimize multitasking is to state a specific period, fifteen minutes for example, to work on a project without interruption, and deal with other tasks afterward. Another way to lessen the risk of staff multitasking during projects is to learn the strengths of team members, what they enjoy most and least about the day-to-day activities, and what environment maximizes their attention and productivity.

Challenge: Choose a Different Approach

1. Identify the repetitive tasks related to a project in your area. Work with your team to come up with some ways to interject an action that breaks through the mundane and adds a bit of spark to the progress. Here are some ideas:
   a. Challenge the team to find one new way to approach a task.
   b. Ring a bell to mark certain levels of completion and have the team cheer.
   c. Schedule ten-minute "refresh" breaks and provide a puzzle or riddle to solve.
2. Have team members take turns handling the repetitive tasks for set periods of time. This gives them mental breaks, prevents focus drift, and supports cross training.

Process Can Inhibit Progress

Make Space for Innovation

Another puzzle revealed this important lesson to me: Sticking to the way I have always done it is not always the best option.

This came into play when I paired up with a new puzzle partner. I discovered that their process was very different from mine. I wanted to start with the outside border, and they wanted to start with the center pieces! I struggled with the idea of straying from the process with which I was most familiar and comfortable. But my approaching every puzzle as just another puzzle to do in my usual way, and not seeing how another perspective might warrant a different approach, left my mind closed and resistant to new and, in this case, a better process.

> The way we have always done it needs to be continually recognized and eliminated.

It turned out that with this round puzzle having a prominent center image, the suggestion for starting in the middle and working outward toward the more abstract sections would prove to be more effective. While both approaches would have eventually achieved the same completion goal, my being flexible in adapting to new ways of doing it helped me develop stronger problem- and process-solving approaches overall. Spend some time seeing yourself in this lesson because in my experience, the way we have always done it is a universal roadblock to adaptability and innovation that needs to be continually recognized and eliminated.

What Does This Teach Us about Leadership?

This is an important lesson in self-reflection that we can all learn from because the-way-we-have-always-done-it mentality is stuck inside habit (either personal or organizational) and is firmly rooted within our comfort zones. Coming from a place where we just want to move forward, stepping out and letting go of the familiar is uncomfortable and learning curves can be awkward. This requires us to place trust in ourselves and in our teams.

This lesson is also connected to leadership and management styles. You may find that the way you have always managed your team members can suddenly become less effective as your team member base changes. You may need to adapt your leadership style to stay aligned with the changing environments of organizational structures and industry directions. In a *Forbes* article titled, "The Most Dangerous Phrase in Business: We've Always Done It This Way," we learn,

> *"As a leader, it is your responsibility to harness a proclivity for adaptation among your employees. I believe it's important to always ask yourself, 'How can I, as a leader, empower my employees to believe in the power of change?'"* [24]

My team experienced this with a new hire on the scene. During a summer staff meeting, we were discussing an already developed and existing supervisor training course that we planned to offer again in the fall. The new team member asked questions about the course and shared some ideas on things we could include that were very different from the way it had always been done. Realizing that this was an important crossroad for the team, I embraced the suggestions and initiated discussion to explore this new way of doing it, thereby allowing the other members of the team to do the same. Just like with the round jigsaw puzzle, if you are open to taking different approaches when appropriate, you can lead your team members through both typical and unexpected challenges and toward pathways to success.

Wellness Perspective

There is great security in the familiar. Perhaps this is even more applicable after the pandemic required changes to many processes, causing significant distress due to the rapid change and ongoing ambiguity. As we worked to adapt, we found that trying new processes may have been disconcerting and took longer at first but became easier

> The way you have always managed your team members can suddenly become less effective as your team member base changes.

and more efficient over time. But even when a new process proves to be more effective or efficient, there remains a strong tendency to revert to what is most familiar.

This provides an excellent opportunity for self-awareness. Noticing how we respond internally to suggestions for using a different method, and defining why we are attached to our approach (habit or that it is, in fact, an effective approach) lends insight into how we make decisions and our level of change tolerance. Deciding how we will respond to, and interact with, others, helps us learn about our communication style and the degree to which our approach builds collaborative relationships.

As Aristotle said: "Knowing yourself is the beginning of all wisdom." This in turn can make us more adaptable and curious about new approaches to standard practices. When we try a new approach and find that it works well, we are more likely to be open to trying new ways of working, while keeping the standard practice

as a foundation. This aspect of personal growth is another contributor to our well-being and life satisfaction.

Challenge: Process Can Inhibit Progress

1. Self-Assess: Explore your habits and patterns for how you
   approach your work. Where do you get set in your ways?
   a. Think of a project you assigned recently. Did you take
      the usual approach, or did you seek out team member
      feedback on the way forward? Where are some other
      areas where you might be set in your ways? What are
      some procedural changes you might make when
      assigning projects in the future?
   b. Practicing different approaches with your own tasks
      helps build and strengthen your adaptability which is a
      critical skill in an any environment.
   c. Respect the tried and true but do not get locked into it.
      The way it has always been done can become a reliable
      backup plan should trying new ways not work as
      planned. Always show gratitude for the new ideas both
      when they work and when they do not.
2. Letting go: The next time you assign a new project, open by
   establishing clear end goals and welcome a discussion with
   your team on different ways of approaching that finish line.
   a. Enter into conversation about their approach and be
      open-minded and curious as to how and why they may
      feel it is the best approach to take.
   b. Give those who will be responsible the flexibility to
      choose what they feel is the best way forward, support
      them along the way, and allow time for the learning
      curve that often accompanies new ways of doing things.
      Follow the advice of Robert Frost whose famous quote
      reminds us that the road less traveled often makes all the
      difference!

Fail Fast - Fail Forward

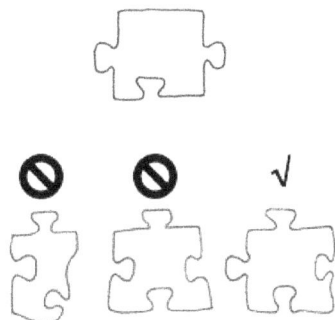

Recognize the Benefits of Try and Try Again

I have never been one to worry too much about trying something and failing. But the lesson of "failing fast" happened when I was in a particularly difficult section of a puzzle where the pattern and color variation made it difficult to find the piece I was looking for. I gathered a handful of pieces that had the colors and shapes that *might* fit, and one by one tried placing them in the empty spot. What I discovered was that, when called for, this technique saves time! The rapid "try and fail" got me to the right piece much faster than the time it would have taken for my eyes to keep scanning the pieces to find the exact one I needed! How often, because we do not want to make a mistake, do we keep delaying action while working it out in our minds until we are absolutely sure that we will get it right or do it right?

Leadership guru John Maxwell advises us to *"Fail early, fail often, but always fail forward."*[25]

Throughout history, making mistakes has been the birthplace of so much forward progress and innovation, yet we still tend to shy away from it because we do not want to look incompetent. As a result, team members will also hesitate to try something different or new for fear of making a mistake and looking incompetent in your eyes.

Here is an example of failing fast and forward. I was facilitating a session on leadership styles and began to provide the instructions for an activity where participants would work in teams to come up with new lyrics to a well-known (or so I thought) tune. The new lyrics would describe the leadership style they were assigned. This had been a popular and fun activity at another organization, but this time it was a failure in the making. Amid a room full of silence and awkward stares, one brave participant informed me that they did not know the song. This was followed by nods all around. I realized that this was a planning failure on my part to know my audience and recognize that given the different cultural demographics this activity would not work for them. I failed forward by quickly coming up with another idea for an activity. I gave them the guidelines for how to write a poem in the haiku format, explaining how the first line of the poem has five syllables, the second line has seven syllables, and the third has five syllables. I challenged them to individually come up with a haiku about their assigned leadership style, and while they worked on theirs, I came up with the following one about my mistake.

> *Looking at blank stares (5)*
> *I can see that I've lost them. (7)*
> *Time to fail forward. (5)*

We were back in gear as they shared their haiku and discussed the pros and cons of the different leadership styles. For me, it reaffirmed two important lessons. The first was the importance of researching my audience and making sure planned activities aligned with their ability to participate. The second was not letting a failure keep me from moving forward quickly.

What Does This Teach Us about Leadership?

Leaders help unlock the potential for innovation by modeling an environment where trying things is encouraged and supported, even when what gets tried fails. When leaders embrace their own failures and share the stories of what happened, what they learned, and how they moved forward, they reinforce support for a culture of exploration and perseverance. By creating an environment where trying, failing, learning from it, and moving forward is encouraged and supported, team members might even produce better results faster! Of course, as with many of these lessons, there will be situations where the failing fast technique poses too high a risk. As leaders, it is important that we encourage and support this technique only where and when appropriate!

Wellness Perspective

When an organization's leaders create an environment where people are not reprimanded for mistakes, but are encouraged to use them as learning opportunities, stress levels are lower. This means people can work more productively and not be fearful of admitting to having made errors.

To create an environment of openness and support, leaders can address the fear of making a mistake and help their team feel empowered to take responsibility for errors without fear of retribution. Many employees place value on professional competence at all costs and have unreasonably high expectations of themselves. Encouraging accountability and self-compassion can help people move forward after an error, as well as strengthen the relationship between a leader and their team.

> Encouraging accountability and self-compassion can help people move forward after an error.

When you realize a mistake has been made, take a few moments to calm your mind and think clearly. Acknowledge the mistake and help determine the causes and contributors. Define what is needed to resolve the issue and inform anyone who needs to know. Approaching errors in a rational manner can improve emotional intelligence and self-confidence and are powerful contributors to well-being and effective leadership.

Challenge: Fail Fast - Fail Forward

1. At a team meeting, present and facilitate discussion about the fail fast - fail forward concept. Start with these discussion prompts:
   a. What does it mean to fail at something?
   b. How is failure avoided?
   c. What fears are triggered when asked to try something that might fail?
   d. What are the benefits (and risks) of trying something that fails?
   e. How do you determine when it is safe to try and fail?
2. Explain the fail-fast-fail-forward concept.
   a. Have the team members discuss when this technique would be an appropriate approach and under what circumstances it would not.
3. Share a personal experience about failing forward.
   a. Share how you learned and moved forward.
   b. Have team members share their experiences with failing forward.

Part Four
Leader as Coach

Focus on Strengths and Interests

Model and Encourage Role Development

Puzzle shapes can represent the various roles that you and your team members are called upon to navigate. By understanding these roles, a leader demonstrates trust and a commitment to team member growth and models a strengths-based leadership approach. Speaker, researcher, and author Brené Brown defines a leader as:

> *"[A]nyone who takes responsibility for finding the potential in people and processes, and who has the courage to develop that potential."* [26]

Team members have roles that they are most comfortable playing, and many have interests in developing within other roles. While one might be most comfortable in facilitating and connecting roles, another might be more comfortable in research and investi-

> Team members have roles that they are most comfortable playing, and many have interests in developing within other roles.

gation roles. For example, when it is time for presentations, look for the communicators who are most comfortable telling a story or sharing information.

Anatomy of a Puzzle Piece

Taking in is focused on connecting with external knowledge and information by being open to new information, ideas, opinions, and perspectives in order to deepen the pool of collective knowledge and lengthen the list of options and alternatives.

- Collaboration
- Active listening
- Facilitation skills
- Curiosity
- Vulnerability

Reaching out is focused on sharing knowledge, information, and perspectives as well as exploring areas of interest or relevance in order to collect and compile information that will contribute in meaningful ways to innovation and goal attainment.

- Research skills
- Presentation skills
- Authenticity
- Creativity
- Communication

Taking these strengths into consideration, leaders can assign tasks and projects in ways that align with their team member's personal strengths and interests. By focusing on skill set combinations that support both the team members and the vision, leaders ensure both team member engagement and forward progress. Think about how workdays take shape based upon the tasks, projects, people, and situations that each week brings. Below, you can see how different puzzle pieces represent the skill set combinations necessary to connect with and share information in various roles.

Facilitate - When bringing team members together, facilitation skills are critical for creating an environment of psychological safety, one where everyone can contribute their ideas and perspectives, innovate new ways forward, or address challenges. Facilitators rely on what everyone can contribute and ensure that all have an opportunity to contribute.

Investigate - Getting all the facts is critical when addressing questions like: "What happened?" "How did it happen?" or "What is the root cause?" The focus is on gathering information and input from customers, colleagues, and stake-holders as well as reviewing timelines, processes, and procedures.

Research - Best suited for those who like to explore what others in the industry are doing. With a focus on "What industry trends are happening?" and "What best practices are out there that can prevent us from reinventing the wheel?" the ability to navigate forums, community pages, research papers, and articles is a must for this role.

Connect - This role networks well in the organization. Because they are well connected, they can be instrumental in bringing people together from different areas to prevent silos and build interdepartmental collaboration.

Communicate - Presenting information with clarity, listening, and fielding questions about a presentation or report takes a high level of subject matter knowledge, interpersonal confidence, and emotional self-control. The message, tone, body language, and an ability to connect with the audience is critical to successful communication.

Collaborate – Look to those who possess a natural ability to work well with others. Good listening skills, an openness to differing ideas, opinions, and perspectives, high levels of respect for colleagues, and a spirit of teamwork is required for this role.

Organize - Overseeing and clarifying boundaries, constraints, and guidelines is a critical role that should not be overlooked when managing people and multiple projects. Keeping things on track, in progress, and on budget requires oversight without overstepping. Delegate someone with strong project management skills.

Understanding the Give and Take

People, like puzzle pieces, are an interesting mix of needs and contributions.

When team members see themselves as an interconnected part of the whole, they can better commit to how they contribute and what they get in return. This is not about work for pay but rather about shared gifts and peer support. Instead of an environment of transaction, it is one of interaction. A relational culture gets things done together. What each team member has to offer and how, as well as how they connect with each other, will vary because each unique piece is positioned to complete a specific place within the big picture.

When you think about your team, think about what you can give them to be successful and recognize what they give to you and to each other in order for you to be successful as a leader. Where your skills in a specific area are weak, theirs might be strong; where your perspective is lacking, they can help broaden it; where they struggle, you can help lift them up. While this should be your dynamic with them, also encourage it in their dynamic with one another.

What happens when a piece gets lost?

It does not happen often, but there have been times when I fit the last available piece into a jigsaw puzzle only to discover an open space in the image. All that work and time spent putting this puzzle together only to see that it is not complete. There is a piece missing.

What Does This Teach Us about Leadership?

As leaders we need to remember that when team members are ready to move on, they are leaving a space to fill a different or bigger space somewhere else where they are needed. What is nice about people rather than puzzle pieces is that there is someone else out there looking to fill the space left behind, someone else who is looking to be the next good fit for your big picture, and that will always be something to celebrate!

Wellness Perspective

Knowing our strengths is an integral step toward career success. This includes leaders first having a solid foundation of understanding their own strengths, and then learning the strengths of each team member. A leader who knows us as individuals rather than just producers of work, who encourages us to define and develop our strengths, and who is adept at pooling the strengths of the team contributes to our well-being because we feel valued and cared for. People can be highly critical of themselves and may focus on weaknesses rather than what they do well. This can erode motivation, and an encouraging, supportive leader can help build our confidence and help us recognize our strengths and find ways to develop them.

According to a 2022 Gallop survey, organizations that focus on identifying and developing team member strengths experience lower rates of burnout and increased engagement [27]. Workplace stressors are not completely eradicated, of course; people are just better able to deal with stress in a healthy manner when the work environment is positive and empowering. Individual and collective well-being in the workplace is enhanced by attention to basic human needs related to maintaining dignity and worth, contributing to higher quality of life.

Challenge: Focus on Strengths and Interests

Unlike puzzle pieces, people are not locked into one way of interconnection. What can you identify as strengths or growing edges in your team members?

1. As you reflect on the pieces described above, identify what you observe as a natural fit for each of your team members.
   a. Some will thrive within multiple roles. What is their greatest strength? Secondary ones?
2. Discuss your observations with each team member.
   a. What strengths do they see in themselves? Do they match or differ from your assessment?
   b. Some may feel they have a strength with limited opportunity to showcase them.
3. Be open to those who identify an interest in other roles as growth opportunities. Seek out opportunities for them to develop in these areas through:
   a. Professional development courses
   b. Mentoring
   c. Job shadowing

Read. Observe. Do. Repeat.

Y ou might not see the situations in the lessons in this book appear in your environment today, tomorrow, or next week. You might read a lesson and think *not my team* or *I don't see that dynamic happening here.* However, at any given time, any one of these situations can appear and require your leadership. People dynamics are complex, and each day brings together a different mix of thoughts, emotions, attitudes, and behaviors into an organization. The more you can understand these dynamics within your circle of influence, the easier it will be for you to lead through the complexities of your work environment. My hope is that you will see the lessons coming, recognize them when they happen, and use them to embrace the amazing dynamics at play in your organization.

This book is not a one and done. It is cyclical.

1. Read the lessons in this book.
2. Observe your environment.
3. Do the challenges.
4. Return to 1.

About the Author

Marjorie J. Loring - MS, PHR, SHRM-CP, QPR

Marjorie is passionate about bringing out the best in people whether they are senior leaders, middle managers, or frontline staff. An optimist, realist, and creative visionary, Marjorie shares techniques which help clients discover and nurture the true potential of their teams with programs and activities that focus on the foundational principles of people management and organizational productivity. With over thirty years of experience in a mix of both corporate and academic settings, Marjorie develops and facilitates seminars, creates customized programs, and partners with internal talent development professionals as a professional learning program consultant. Learn more at kindlingleadership.com.

"My purpose is to facilitate the sharing of knowledge, perspectives, and experiences so that it can support mutual growth, strengthen connections, and build trust within and across communities."

Wellness Contributor

Lisa Elsinger - PhD, CMBM, QPR

Lisa is a passionate and caring leader, coach, collaborator, facilitator of lifelong learning and growth, and community-builder, moving through life with diligence, grace, and gratitude. Through her Live Well program, she promotes individual and collective well-being, applying the dimensions of wellness using a social ecological model framework. As a workplace wellness visionary Lisa leads comprehensive population health and well-being initiatives, employee experience programming, and strategies to maintain an engaging work climate. Having moved beyond traditional wellness programs, her work contributes to a culture where people feel acknowledged, valued, and a sense of belonging.

"My purpose is to share insights, information, and inspiration that helps people care for their well-being so that they can live life with energy, vitality, and fulfillment of their aspirations."

Endnotes

1 Simon Sinek, *The Infinite Game* (2021)

2 https://en.wikipedia.org/wiki/Self-determination_theory

3 Michael McKinney, "Developing a Small-Wins Strategy for Growth," *Leading Blog* (June 23, 2010), https://www.leadershipnow.com/leadingblog/2010/06/developing_a_smallwins_strateg_1.html

4 Debbie Cohen and Kate Roeske Zummer, *Humanity Works Better* (Vancouver: Page Two Books, Inc., 2021,) 37

5 "State of the Global Workplace: 2023 Report," Gallup, 2023, https://www.gallup.com/workplace/349484/state-of-the-global-workplace.aspx

6 John Maxwell, *The 21 Irrefutable Laws of Leadership* (Harper Collins, 2022), https://www.azquotes.com/quote/549458

7 Carol Henry, "7 Ways to Grow as a Leader," | Carol Henry Coaching retrieved May 8, 2023, https://carolhenry coaching.com/2018/08/06/7-ways-to-grow-as-a-leader/

8 Paul J. Zak, "The Neuroscience of Trust," *Harvard Business Review* (January-February 2017): 84-90, https://hbr.org/2017/01/the-neuroscience-of-trust

9 Jody Michael, "Why We Need to Celebrate Minor Milestones," *Forbes* (Sept. 20, 2021), https://www.forbes.com/sites/forbescoachescouncil/2021/09/20/why-we-need-to-celebrate-minor-milestones/?sh=53df7ec85ae8

10 Kendra Cherry, "Self Efficacy and Why Believing in Yourself Matters," verywellmind, updated February 27, 2023, https://www.verywellmind.com/what-is-self-efficacy-2795954

11 Ranstad, The Benefits of Diversity in Building Teams (Sept. 4, 2020), https://www.randstad.ca/employers/workplace-insights/talent-management/the-benefits-of-building-diverse-teams/

12 Evan Leybourn, "Adopting Pair Work," Business Agility Institute (Feb. 26, 2019), https://businessagility.institute/learn/adopting-pair-work/158

13 Courtney E. Ackerman, "Self Determination Theory and How it Explains Motivation," *Positive Psychology* (June 21, 2018), https://positivepsychology.com/self-determination-theory/

14 Jacqui Barrett-Poindexter, "How to Encourage Your Employees to Own Their Individual Value in a Teamwork Environment," Glassdoor for Employers (June 7, 2017), https://www.glassdoor.com/employers/blog/how-to-encourage-your-employees-to-own-their-individual-value-in-a-teamwork-environment/

15 McKinsey & Company, "It's not about the office, its about belonging" (Jan. 13, 2022), https://www.mckinsey.com/capabilities/people-and-organizational-performance/our-insights/the-organization-blog/its-not-about-the-office-its-about-belonging

16 U.S. Department of Health and Human Services, "U.S. Surgeon General Releases New Framework for Mental Health & Well-Being in the Workplace" (Oct. 20, 2022), https://www.hhs.gov/about/news/2022/10/20/us-surgeon-general-releases-new-framework-mental-health-well-being-workplace.html#:~:text=Mattering at Work: People want

17 U.S. Department of Health and Human Services, "U.S. Surgeon General's Framework for Workplace Mental Health & Well-Being" (Oct. 20, 2022),

https://www.hhs.gov/sites/default/files/workplace-mental-health-well-being.pdf

18 Melissa Eisler, "A Strategic Leadership Paradox: Slow Down to Speed Up" (Jan. 20, 2021) https://widelensleadership.com/slow-down-to-speed-up/

19 Karl Halvor Teigen, "Yerkes-Dodson: A law for all seasons," Theory & Psychology 4, no. 4 (1994): 525–547, https://doi.org/10.1177/0959354394044004

20 Rebecca Noori, "Work Overload: What Is It and How to Avoid it on Your Team" (updated June 7, 2023). https://timelyapp.com/blog/work-overload

21 Elizabeth Grace Saunders, "6 Causes of Burnout, and How to Avoid Them," *Harvard Business Review* (July 5, 2019), https://hbr.org/2019/07/6-causes-of-burnout-and-how-to-avoid-them

22 Tork, "Take Back the Lunch Break Survey Findings" (2018), https://workplace.msu.edu/breaks-during-the-workday/#:~:text=Taking breaks throughout the workday,burnout and higher stress levels

23 Jaewon Yoon et al., "How to Make Even the Most Mundane Tasks More Motivating," *Harvard Business Review* (July 24, 2019), https://hbr.org/2019/07/how-to-make-even-the-most-mundane-tasks-more-motivating?registration=success

24 Ben Zimmerman, "The Most Dangerous Phrase in Business: We've Always Done It This Way," *Forbes* (Jan. 28, 2019), https://www.forbes.com/sites/forbeslacouncil/2019/01/28/the-most-dangerous-phrase-in-business-weve-always-done-it-this-way/?sh=6d33a8dd40f7

25 John C. Maxwell, *Failing Forward* (Harper Collins, 2007) 176

26 Brené Brown, *Dare to Lead* (Random House, 2018), https://brenebrown.com/hubs/dare-to-lead/

27 "State of the Global Workplace: 2023 Report," Gallup, 2023, https://www.gallup.com/workplace/349484/state-of-the-global-workplace.aspx

www.ingramcontent.com/pod-product-compliance
Lightning Source LLC
Chambersburg PA
CBHW050512210326

41521CB00011B/2420